Musings of a Stone-Cold Genius

Volume 1

by R.D. Gilliam

2024

Cover design by R.D. Gilliam

Stone-Cold Press
P.O. Box 2489
Danville, Ky 40423

Printed in the United States of America

Copyright: RD Gilliam, 2024   ISBN 979-8-9908808-0-1

All rights reserved. No part of this book may be used or reproduced by any means, graphic, electronic, or mechanical, including photocopying, taping, and recording without written permission.

Table of Contents

    Introduction 1
    Caution 2
    Pretty Little Flowers 3
    Nightfall 4
    Baptized 5
    Carry You 6
    Music 7
    Daisies 8
    Do You 9
    Grace of the Fall 10
    Folly 11
    Waiting 12
    The Storm 13
    Butterfly 14
    Ready 15
    A Moment in Mind 16
    Good Morning 17
    Blind 18
    Candlelight 19
    Care 20
    Midnight Eyes 21
    Foolishness 22

Kaleidoscope of Life	23
Itch	24
Where Am I	25
Rescue	26
Up To You	27
Rotting Roses	28
Rain Dance	29
Wind	30
Chasing Rainbows	31
Steps	32
Bite	33
The Dream	34
Crown	35
Dance	36
My Friend	37
Unexpected	38
Black is the Day	39
I Dance Alone	40
Into the Fire	41
See	42
Dream a Dream	43
The Key	44
4	45
Head of the Room	46

I Don't Fight 47
Web 48
Flying 49
Soul Surfer 50
War 51
Tenant Farmer 52
Fight 53
Your Magic 54
Stardust 55
High 56
Lady 57
Rain 58
Country Stream 59
The Exchange 60
Fit 61
Little Badass 62
Beast 63
Glory 64
Vapor 65
Lull Prayer 66
Granny's Table 67
? 68
Elixir 69
Light the Night 70

In His Eyes 71
What Spills From Me 72
What She was Given 73
My Body 74
Time 75
Fucking People 76
Ailments of the Human Condition 77
Rain 78
Simple People 79
The Cover of Night 80
My Love 81
Lovely is the Day 82
21 Day Challenge 83
Author Bio 93

Introduction

Thank you, Shawn, for supporting all my ventures. Thank you, Tyler and Sarah, Winston and Racheal, Reed and Myranda, Tucker, Robot, Juju, Winnie, Wilton, Amory, Aeary and Auron, you're the very best family, ever. Thank you **bunches** Momma. Thanks to the rest of my family, you mean the world to me. Thank you to my friends, I'm lucky to have each of you in my life.

Thank you Paul Stansbury for helping me get this done! You're awesome! Check Paul out at www.paulstansbury.com.

This book of little writings is dedicated to my Dad who I'm sure would say, "That's alright kid" and be very proud of me.

Names have been changed to protect the innocent as well as the guilty. Credit to whomever said it first, it sure wasn't me.

Any resemblance to other works or persons is strictly coincidental.

Also, I feel it prudent to tell readers that while I did write all this very little is about me. It's all from me but not all about me. I have things constantly churning in my mind. It's just always there, always on. My thoughts flow and run and jump and skip and crawl and any other adjective you can use for movement. I just let them go…..in every direction and I don't censor it. Plenty of it is thought for character development for a novel I sure hope to publish someday. Some of it's about me, some of it's about people I know, plenty of it is just shit in my head.

R. D. Gilliam

Caution

If you're bothered by misspellings, poor grammar, incorrect sentence structure and over all randomness…..
Stop now.
Go take your meds.
Maybe get a snack and use the restroom. Give those meds time to kick in.
Then come back to this.

Pretty Little Flowers

Water the pretty little flowers
The ones who need pots and shelter
Help them grow
Set them in the sun
So that they may thrive
Talk to the pretty little flowers with love
and sing them lullabies
Rub the dust from their tiny leaves
Let them play in the warm misty rain
So that they feel the lightness of joy
Give them all the love and fertilizer they need to grow
To flourish
To become giants
Yes
water the pretty little flowers and watch their beautiful colors bloom

Nightfall

I love nightfall
The changing of the guard
Especially when the air is crisp
The sound of water rolling along
There's a certain energy
It radiates from the air
The ground
Me
I feel alive
I feel electric
I feel apart of

Baptized

    Last night I sat in the rain and let it wash my sins away. I didn't pray for forgiveness or absolution, could that even be found. I just sat there with my head low, tired and ugly until my mind went black.

    The warm rain beat down my back but I felt it on my soul. Hundreds of little stinging pricks chipping away at my stain. Whether the pain was gone or I'd just grown accustomed to it I don't know, but I could no longer feel the sting.

    So I sat there numb in the rain watching it drip from my hair, my nose, my fingers. I watched it swirl in little pools around the gravel willing myself to be the rain. Of course, that was in vain. I could never be the rain. So finally, after an amount of time I'd lost measure of, I lifted my head, pulled my shoulders back and went inside.

Carry You

If I'm never in your arms again
Will you remember my skin
And the way we were then

Your memory burns bright
warms my soul from within
I see you there but I feel you here
in the space just for you
the space in me

when the wind calls my name
and I trade this ache for pain
will you remember my touch
and how my smile meant so much

I still feel you
In my heart
In my mind
In my soul
I carry you

Music

The melody wraps around me like a soft blanket
Snuggling into the soft warmth I move side to side
forward and back
Notes push and pull and sway my body until I move on instinct
Muscle and bone move as the music speaks my soul and spills my heart
To fight this feeling is not an option
Rise and fall, the floor cool to my feet
notes float in the air as candlelight dances along as if it can't help it's self either
slicing through the still night to give it movement and purpose
This moment, this single moment, is the most lovely and I shall stay in it, in my heart.

Daisies

Under a field of daisies
My pleasure it does lie
Once I strolled the daisies free
But now unrest fills in me
The days I do not reside
Within my field of pride
Longing fills my belly full
Until my path is once again
Beneath the daisy field

Do You

I'll give you one, two, three guesses why
The world can't be contained by the beautiful sky
The world is you and the world is me
Turns out we're all community
But there's only a few
A very great few
Who see with their hearts what's meant to be
To play in the snow and stomp puddles dry
To get lost in the chase of a blue butterfly
Did you forget that feeling so fine
Or do you dance with the rain in a zig zag line

Grace of the Fall

Is there anything more beautiful than a women's fall from grace?
Not in society's eyes but in her own.
When she gives over to desire and need and no longer clings to decency.
I speak not of that soulless giving out of loneliness or emptiness or often self-loathing.
That's common.
Oh no, that sad pathetic fall is altogether different.
No, I mean the one when she truly surrenders her soul because nothing of her being will allow her to hold it.
It's more rare than you'd think, this fall.
It's beautiful and shines and glows with warmth and fire and things long whispered about in the dark.
I'm not sure it's often recognized by the one she spilled herself for and what a shame it is to miss such a beautiful fall.

Folly

Trust me there will be no one there to catch you
You look for a net
squint your eyes until there's a permanent crease marking your hope
But you'll mash your face every time
You fool
Don't you get tired of meeting the ground
It doesn't kiss softly yet you never learn
Still you leap
Or stumble and fall over rocks you clearly see
Most of the time you even enjoy your fall
Lift your face to the heavens and smile
Fool
But goddam that ground
It's an unforgiving bed

Waiting

Into the night I steal away
The wild calling me
I used to fight the instinct
But now I give it free reign
To take me places I've never been
And to some I've been too many times
I was empty for a while and couldn't see the light
But here in the dark I see so clearly the true color of me
My mind is free and my soul soars high
On a wicked wind I fly
I see those below who do not know but I have no time for pity
One day they'll see or slip away and never be
Day breaks quiet to some but thunders in my ears
I slide back in and hide away
Waiting for my time to see

The Storm

I stood silent and still in the window watching the storm pitch it's fit
Throwing lightening jabs and wind punches while the thunder roared it's madness
The rain poured down like angry tears that wouldn't be staved
I knew how that storm felt, I'd been there many times
This storm a sister to my soul
Tomorrow or the next day or the next after that
there'd be sun to shine a light on the wreckage and destruction
the glorious aftermath
To give rest and reprieve before the next storm lays her vengeance down
A new beginning to a new day
Some would ask, "Can we appreciate the sunshine if we never knew the storm?"
I stand silent in the window watching the storm and think, "I hope you see the beauty in both."

Butterfly

How many cocoons must we have before we become the butterfly?
Can we not build our shelter and slumber until our wings unfurl?
That's not the way of us
We're a roadblock to our higher selves
Constructing what looks like existence should look to half blind eyes
Building a cage of greed and low level thinking to point in which we cannot rest
Cannot grow
Cannot transform
We cannot be the butterfly
And it's all at our own construct
Construction of our own destruction How pitiful we are
We could each be great
Not of wealth
Or power
Or fame
But of person

Ready

Why is the day so goddamned long
But the night is gone in an instant
The minutes just crawling by numb and at times torturous in their slow tediousness
The torture almost better than the numb
At least pain stands up to be counted
But when darkness comes to swallow the day I can breathe
Hours fly by like seconds
Elation takes the place of pain and a smile graces my face, just seconds ago ugly with apathy
Turning it to thing of almost beauty
Stone moves like water and dances like fire
Others watch the spectacle and wonder what possession has hold of me
It's in your eyes
The unholy and how you hate
You don't understand
You can't play with me child you're not ready

A Moment in Mind

Walking around in circles day after day
year after year
ignorant to life
Ignorant to what life could be
All these people I watch every day
I don't know if I pity them or envy them
Both, I think, depending on the day
It isn't so easy as pity or envy, not really
Days I loathe
Days I laugh
Days I love
Most days I just observe
Looking for more
Looking to learn
I can't help but study the wonder of people

Good Morning

There's no light beaming through the window, not yet. It's still dark, still my time. I lay in the quiet dark enjoying the in and out of air in my lungs, the lub dub of my heart and the warmth gathering between my legs as I think of you. My breathing deepens to match the want building in me. Did I lick my lips? I must have, I feel the wetness cooling in the predawn air. I breathe just little heavier still and notice the feel of the sheet against my pebbled nipples, more sensitive than they were just seconds ago. I feel the pressure between my legs, but I don't touch myself. Not yet. I love the sweet agony of waiting. I recall the way your fingertips moved slowly, softly from thigh to hip, then around my waist, up the middle of my back. More firmly now, your touch, as you press those same fingertips into my shoulder. It's harder now not to touch myself. As I think about how your hardness felt against my leg. I want to touch you so badly I ache. To feel you pressed to me. Your hot, unyielding touch, relentless in your pursuit of my pleasure. I can stand it no longer and run my finger from my thigh to my sex, touching ever so gently to tease even farther the fire I can't put out but only hope to smother the blaze for a time. I lovingly stroke myself pulling my moisture up. Up to the spot where I'll see blind color in a fit of madness, with an image of you in my mind, the mingling taste of you and me on my lips. My whole body moves on it's own, I couldn't control it or stop it now if I wanted to. Ecstasy literally at my fingertips. With moans and grunts and sounds not exactly pretty, I spill over the edge. Life and love and sex and need and every delicious sin I need, I spasm and fall through myself. And so begins another glorious day.

Blind

I lost sight
I thought my eyes were steady and clear
Somehow the blurred lines went unnoticed and became normal to me
Once I had purpose, a goal, a mission but I lost sight
And while I was blind, I lost my way
Stumbled along a familiar path I thought I'd cleared
Little stumbles on life pebbles
tree roots grabbing my feet to plant my face in the dirt
Mud puddles that look like fun until I walk miles with soaking feet
I stop
I feel my folly
The comedy of me
I close my blind eyes and just breathe
Feel the world around me
My world
The things along my path simply are *Life*
With my eyes still closed, my breathing deep and calm, I see it clearly again
The path is what I make it
When I want to stomp puddles, I will
When I want to walk streets of diamonds and gold, I will
When I want fire for light, I'll see it so
When I want silent moonlight strolls, I'll flirt with the man in the moon
When I stumble and fall I'll see
I'll see the truth of my fall, the truth of me.
Maybe get right back up
Maybe I'll crawl
Maybe I'll lay flat on my back and watch the stars
Whatever I so choose.

Candlelight

By Candlelight I see desire dance across your face
Warm and glowing
Predatory
No place to hide
Not even in the shadows moving about
I can sense if I run I'll just be caught
Eaten alive
Left in pieces
It's instinctual to lower my eyes to you
To bow my head
To offer my neck
Still I fight the instinct
It's foreign to me
I don't know how to lower my eyes
I've never before felt a soul my match
I stand paralyzed
By fear?
Not for myself, of that I'm sure
By hope?
Maybe this one's for me, I'd hate to fail here

Care

Apathy
What a hideous state to exist in
Absurd really
To live without passion
Who would want that
I've allowed myself to slide into apathy a time or 2
What a waste
I suppose it may be the fruit of inattention to one's self
Don't let apathy be your color
Be passionate
About anything
About something

Midnight Eyes

Midnight eyes don't inspire poetry
Midnight eyes don't write songs
Midnight eyes don't bring men to their knees
Midnight eyes aren't looked into in awe of their beauty
Midnight eyes hide
Midnight eyes hide a soul that longs
Midnight eyes hide a heart that bleeds
Midnight eyes hide a mind that dreams
Midnight eyes hide a strength so strong it's a weakness

Foolishness

Damn my romantic nature
I hide it so well for the most part
I try hardest to hide it from myself
But I'm a fool you see
Just foolish enough to hope
That's what romantics do you know
We hope
For something grand
And beautiful
Something beyond reason
Beyond logic
That hope swells and blooms and smells beautiful in our mind
And we float on that hope
Until reality pricks our bubble
Until truth writes it's name along our belly
Then we're left in a puddle of our own bloody foolishness.
An ocean sized puddle sometimes
I should let go of the string that holds me to hope,
That foolish silly hope,
And let the darkness take me
It's where I belong

Kaleidoscope of Life

Life is really a funny thing
An amazing thing
It's always changing
Maybe in tiny little measurements
so small you barely notice
Then one day you look around and the stores and restaurants you knew so well
in earlier years have been replaced with new businesses you now know so well
But one day they to will be replaced
You barely noticed they spilled into history and not that those changes are bad
Some are, some aren't but they just sort of happen without much notice
But Life, it's a funny thing
Sometimes the change is sudden, staggering
Your whole world shifts
The patterns are all new
The colors all different
You have to check each step because the terrain shifted right under your feet
Still this big change may be good or bad and different for each of us
It's a crazy thing we don't stand in awe of the evolution of Life
Evolution of our way of life
What a lovely little journey

Itch

What is this thing that crawls beneath my skin?
That torments me day and night
Ever present with its insistence to be noticed but never dealt with
I can't dig it out
The thing moves about finding new hiding places when I get close to laying fingers on its wriggly mass
It's almost a friend now, my constant companion
I might even miss it if I actually cut it out
When it's still and I feel only the burden of it's presence and not the itch it likes to make
I wonder what soothed this demon for a measure
Or is it soothed at all
Dread starts to seep inside my belly
One day it's going to bite me
I feel it sure as I feel the ground at my feet
Maybe start eating at me until I'm gone
No longer even real
Just a ghost of myself

Where Am I

I belong in the dungeon alongside criminals and rats
Somewhere dirty and smelly
Maybe a loathsome rapist wallows in his own shit, not worthy of a pot
spiders crawl about the old bastard in the night and try to make their way to me
No sun to be felt on my face or soothing water running nearby to float my woes away
No just darkness and maybe not even the company of the terrible, rotting rapist for possible connection
Just left in the cold, damp darkness to run from rats and such
Still I sit here on the soft, warm grass with the breeze rustling my hair, the smell of honeysuckle in my nose with the sun warming my cold soul.
How is this?
Someone so dark as me can't surely be above ground to feel the feels and smell the smells
To love the loves
Can this be so? I dare to hope.
I'll to be crushed in an instant
To find a cruel trick the Gods play
To find my sun is only a dream

Rescue

I could just choke on all the perfectly placed, pretty, warm home, bullshit sitting about
I suppose when your world is so fucked up all you have is the pretend
A Norman Rockwell for your eyes when your insides are eaten up with ugliness it's all you've got
Most of the time I feel sorry for your pathetic life
How much you care what others think
Some days it pisses me off
I get pissed at myself for even giving you a second of my goddamn time
The overly sweet perfection of your existence makes me sick
Give me the fucking gutter any day
Where the rats are real and the piss stinks

Up To You

Everyone has damage,
it's just a fact of life.
My damage may be different than yours but we both still have it.
But we both have flowers in our garden too.
Tiny little blooms or big, vibrant perfuming flowers.
We both have those as well.
People are people
That's all I'm saying
So it's up to you
if you feel sorry for yourself
If you waller in your shit
See if that helps you any
Maybe it will
Just spread that fertilizer around and grow some more flowers

Rotting Roses

    I see your world over there. Such a shiny , lovely place, all sunshine and roses. You're pretty, perfect smile beams bright, bringing all to your feet. Beautiful blonde hair brushes softly across your fair peachy skin and floats effortless on the soft warm breeze. Oh how beautiful your world is. Your pretty little house with bushes and roses lined perfectly for the world to see. To see how good your life can be. And for a second, just a handful of seconds, I want that perfect world too. To let only the sun shine on me. But I know that's not for me. I can't live there. That's only a daydream really. An illusion. Over in my world, the place you fear the most, it rains. The wind blows with fury, whipping my wild dark hair at every angle. My eyes fierce with knowledge and truth, I see it all. Teeth bared in a growl, a warning to any who might come near. I could pretend to be like you but rather I'll be true. I'll see the sun when it shines, the rain when it falls and the roses when they rot. And when darkness takes my world I grin a little then. See I walk with wolves in silver light and dance with fairies in the night.

Rain Dance

      I dance in the rain. He sees me there but won't take my hand. I long to share this feeling but he can't see the magic here. The splendor of drops falling down on me and the tiny mist of rebound rain, butterfly kisses. And I'm just sure if he'd take my hand he'd feel the kisses too. Still he stands on the porch looking at me with confusion and maybe a touch of fear. I reach again, trying to coax him out to me but he stands there as a Shepard's tree just staring out at me. The drum beat I hear comes straight from my soul, the very core of me. So loudly I feel it, I don't understand how he can't feel it too. I close my eyes and feel the beat and the rain and the wind and I dance and I dance and I dance. And then I dance some more. I open my eyes and try to see him but I've dance myself away.

Wind

Wind in my face at every turn
North wind
South wind
East wind
West wind
I can't say I don't deserve the opposition
I just don't fucking want it
I could easily say fuck it and close myself in
but where's the fun in that
So I twist my head to the sky and scream from my gut
"FUCKING BLOW ME AWAY!!!!"

Chasing Rainbows

    Sitting in the room with the others I knew in my core we were not the same. Pretty little lives just sprinkled all about. Oh they have their troubles, everyone does, but their minds are so black and white it makes their world small. Tidy. Tidy little lives they live. Even the ones who look untidy are aware they live in the black part of the picture but even still their mess is small and tidy.

    Where do I live? In the grey. Chasing rainbows.

Steps

      The land was frozen and barren with a wind that whipped tiny ice daggers at my face. A world free of color and warmth, having only shades of grey. The light came and went but never showed warmth or even a source. One foot in front of the other, step by step, around boulders, over hills and mountains. I don't even know why I'm walking but I do. If I stop to rest I'm giving up somehow. Giving up something of myself. Forward I march through some amount of time that's indistinguishable. Through an amount of space I can't begin to measure. So without a compass, without a reason, without a purpose I take these tiny little ice bites to my face. I'm past being weary. I'm desolate and for the thousandth time I think "What is this God forsaken place?" And with my question this time comes the answer. Hell. Relief washes over me and I breathe easy for the first time. I made this hell I'll burn the motherfucker down.

Bite

To be special to someone
What a childish thing to want
Most of us want it and maybe some people find it
The pretty people
Maybe they find it
But when you're the ugly truth no one wants to face
You don't find it
You find armor and barricades and walls to put your back against
And you keep fighting even when the enemy retreats Snarl and snap
A Fair warning to all
"You best get back."

The Dream

I long to see your skin in the morning light, little dust particles whirling in the air above you. The rise and fall of your chest as you lay heavy in sleep sets my breathing to yours. My natural inclination is to match you, I do it without thought. I watch and breathe and breathe and watch until I can no longer stop my lips. They have to taste your skin. A soft kiss just outside your pit, it's the closest place to me as my head rests on your shoulder. Then another little kiss because I can't help myself. I feel your hand tighten just a little on my hip. I don't want you to wake, not just yet, so I still my lips. When your breathing evens out again I lay awhile longer feeling the length of you against the length of me hoping to keep you like this a little longer. But I can stand it no longer yet again so I trace languid, soft kisses across your skin in an effort to keep you asleep. I see your body stir to life and know I wasn't gentle enough to keep you in the dream.

Crown

My soul floats on the breeze
Carried through time and space
As large as the universe
As light as the dandelion seed
I let chaos choose my path today
As circumstance is my nature
But when I step down
To take my crown
Beware the night's calm
For gone is the easy breeze of day

Dance

Ghosts of time play symphonies in my mind
Taking turns at the crescendo in an effort to tire me out
But my blood beats fast and hot
I won't let these haunts still me
Oh no, for as fast and loud as you can play
I will match you in my dance

My Friend

She was a pretty little thing, all the boys tried to catch her eye. Long, silky blonde hair, big saucer blue eyes, dimples for days. And the girls, they all wanted to be her. Every little girl wants to be Miss America and they all could see she was a Miss America. Some were openly mean while others sat pretending to be her friend all the while being mean when her eyes were turned. She smiled at them most of the time, she didn't know what else to do. But the one girl, she was different. She wasn't mean and didn't pretend. She just became her friend.

Unexpected

Unexpected you came into my life
I see the world in your eyes
One touch from you and my whole world crumbled
I'm hypnotized
Lost
Please take my hand
Lets walk this land
You and I in the dance of life
Our way
What more could anyone want?

Black is the Day

Love has left me exhausted
You set me up to be a villain when you put me on a Princess's pedestal
Look deep into my wicked eyes and see the truth of me
I could sooner be the thorn on a rose
than be a pretty, perfect bloom
My mind is wicked
My heart is black and if there was ever good in me
It's been crushed out by the weight of expectation
Try as I might to wear the princess crown
My head can no longer carry it's tiny weight
I lay upon the cold, cold floor, fallen weary and worn

I Dance Alone

I dance alone

When midnight strikes and lovers reach for one another

I dance alone

When the sun shines and the fields are bright with daisies and children run free with glee

I dance alone

When the sky opens and spills tears of life soaked up by the dusty earth

I dance alone

With each rotation in life and time

I dance alone

But in my next life, oh in my next life

I'll dance with you.

Into the Fire

Into the fire
Burning and blistering
Not consumed by it
Oh no the flames work to match our energy
We are the fire
Elevated
Our heat to warm the world

See

I close my eyes and open my mind
Blue explodes to the front
Beautiful
Intense
Full of fun
Crystal clear with knowledge and purpose
I'd spend a lifetime in those stormy seas but I haven't learned
to swim
I reach for a helping hand
Someone to teach me how to stay afloat
No hand
No life raft
No way to gain purchase
Blue lets me face to black

Dream a Dream

I lay in a field of daisies and little purple flowers
the earth's scent filling my nose
Blue sky and fluffy white clouds float above making pictures lost to time
Have I been happy before this moment?
I'm sure I have but this moment is so full of the peace
I can't seem to find or remember from other times
My mind stills
my body relaxes and calm washes over me.
Do you smell the earth too?
Do you see pictures in the clouds?
Do you love?
Do you, Love

The Key

It's so easy to eat the lies
Bitter taste of deceit hidden beneath the sweet
Turn back into yourself
Listen to your voice
Your conscious thought led by your spirit
Let you guide the way
They built a box and you walked right in
Sat down on a fluffy sofa and waited for the saccharine to be served
Ate it down in gluttonous bites
Cozy there in your righteous seat
Sucking propaganda's tit
Sucking so long you forgot the door
Didn't even check to see
Hell you haven't glanced out the window to even wish for more
You forgot to think
You forgot to live your way
But here's the thing
It's so important to see, to the door that isn't even locked
There is a key

4

It's 4 in the morning
Oh lord my heart is sick
It's 4 in the morning
Oh lord my soul is weak
I been sittin' here so long
I can't even move my feet
It's 4 in the morning
Oh lord you know I try
See the devil has me by the toe
and dances at my side
Peace just don't know my name
Yes the devil has me by the soul
And peace I just don't know

Head of the Room

Look to the head of the room
you'll see the true King
He's easy to spot
Not by his crown
Not by his ring
or even by his sword
He doesn't sit his throne
he rides it
Ever vigilant
at the ready
with determination in his eyes

I Don't Fight

    Awakened again at 4 a.m., this surely is my witching hour. I'm uneasy, unsettled, there's something I need to do. Clumsily I dress and make my way downstairs to pour a finger of my favorite burn. But tonight I don't stand at the counter to drink. Not tonight. The night calls me out. With a blanket around my shoulders and liquid comfort in my hand I take my seat on the cold hard step and gaze out into the night. The air's cold as fuck but I'm filled with an energy I'm sure is from the divine. My mind and body alive with knowledge and awareness my soul is called away to a place of peace I rarely find. I found it tonight because in this moment I don't fight. I don't fight my demons. I don't fight my solitude. I don't fight my dark nature. I don't fight that I crave life. I don't fight that I'm sensual. I don't fight that I'm unusual. I don't fight that I'm more than most will ever know.

Web

When was I innocent? I can barely remember the time. Maybe I never was but surely that time has passed and I didn't even realize I had it in the first place. Not at the time but now I can pinpoint the moment it evaporated, what innocence I had, and safety left my world. See I'm armed with knowledge that most don't have and I never thought to be bothered by it all. As someone before me said, "what's normal to the spider is chaos to the fly. I've been the spider and I've been the fly. These days I'm the web.

Flying

Lovely is the soul that lives with abandon for the wind calls and the answer trips along the leaves. The spirit rests in beautiful nests to be born and fly again. And if you're lucky you'll see that spirit flying by. If you're willing to try you can climb up high and dive off into the wind.

Soul Surfer

Beneath the surface lies a hole that only the reflection hides
a vast expanse ready to swallow up all
Not a void so that everything is lost
but a space that grows and lives by life's lessons learned
An energy so great and wide most can't withstand the pressure but once in a
while a soul dives in to swim the depths and ride the current free

War

    Born behind your defenses an invisible enemy attacks. Silently invading, raising no alarms. Sneaking down paths like a criminal in the night. Who would expect the enemy to be your own. Already in a war you didn't even know you were in, you rise for the day, drink your coffee, eat breakfast, go to work, talk about things you think are important, wondering why you're so tired. You clean your house, tend the garden, make supper or whatever your day looks like, you go about it until the silent enemy has attacked and invaded so much it's silence now a scream. You wake up on the floor, having passed out and lain there for hours. So the first battle of the war you didn't know you were in begins.

Tenant Farmer

Looking out across the land he'd worked for half his life the old man let out a sigh. His time in the field had come to an end and just like any other broken tool he'd been cast aside. He should go help his wife with the packing but his body is still too weak. He doesn't look at the future but tries hard to make it to the next hour. Life's been a series of uneventful choices that landed him here and now. By days end he lies on the floor, hurting, past tired and weary. Hand thrown across his scared forehead, he can't even open his eyes to see his family. His years too short and quite unkind. I lay down beside him in the floor and yammer on about who knows what, most likely a puppy. He just smiles a little. He rarely told me no.

Fight

    I can't lay down my sword and shield. In my bones I know my enemy is gone, no longer lurking in the shadows but my mind won't let me see the darkness is empty of the monsters. Still defending. Still protecting. Still vigilant. I long to rest and find the peace I've never known. If I ever knew it the memory is so distant, I've lost it long ago. Forward I march, seeking my safe place. The place where I can rest. I know this place rests in my mind and seems closer than I've ever known before, but I'm lost. I can't find my way through the veil. It keeps moving on me, that passage to the safe side. Just out of my reach. In my peripheral but when I turn to look it's not there. Cruel tricks the gods play on me for entertainment. I'll fight them too if that's what I have to do. Gods and demons and monsters in shadows, I'll fight you all, which of you makes me no matter.

Your Magic

    Your voice echoes around my mind and twines it's way around my heart to my very core and while they aren't my own they somehow belong to me. Seems I feel the pain and love and hunger as though they are my own. So I close my eyes, rest my head and go along for the ride. Such a beautiful trip, bright with magic and light that most don't seem to know but radiates so easily through your every note.

Stardust

    Sitting at the table surrounded by friends, laughing and joking and smiling, no one sees she's alone. Oh her smile is genuine, it reaches her eyes, she's having fun with the people as she communes but she's alone. When she lays down beside her lover later that same night, even as he strokes her face, she's alone. While feeding her elderly neighbor with nothing but good will in her heart, she's alone. When she's so high she hears the angels sigh, she's alone. Through every deed, light and dark alike, she's alone. She once believed the fairytale that told her there was more in store and one pretty day she'd be alone no more. That story was a Grim for sure. Even through love she was alone. Always alone. A beautiful golden light split the grey and the girl knew if she could feel the light upon her skin she would know togetherness. It was so close she could feel it's warmth but the golden beam stayed just out of reach and the girl was forever alone. Last life, this life, next life, a lonely, solitary piece of stardust.

High

Let's get high. Oh, come on. You know you want to. To feel that blissful haze of "no fucks to give" roll over. That sweet spot when shit just can't touch you. When the memory of a summer night so long ago floats in on the breeze and stirs up a hurricane of shit. But it's ok because you're high and shit don't matter. Your mind slows down so you can enjoy the colors dancing in your eyes, painting a picture of a time and place where your soul rests. Oh, come on now, let's get high. That peace is found in the hazy high and if anyone tells you it's somewhere else you know they're a fuckin' lie. Go on pick your poison and get the deed done. You know the whole world will still be waiting when you come down.

Lady

Hold the door for me
Pull out my goddamn chair
Rest your hand on the small of my back so the room knows I'm yours
Am I not precious?
Do I not sparkle enough for you?

But he looked.
He sees
He doesn't look away
He can't look away
I don't know what others see
Shimmers maybe
He sees a diamond

Rain

My time in the rain was glorious. Why do people dislike the rain so much? It's nourishing and sexy, the way the beads of water run down your skin. I feel alive and fresh and bursting with energy. Puddle splashing and rain dancing feed my soul with the most basic of things, joy. Connected to everything, that's how it feels to dance in the rain. And the world is so bright and pretty with growth, a feast for your starving eyes. Just slow down and take a look, you'll see, time spent in the rain yields beautiful blooms.

Country Stream

I long to be a country stream
flowing with quiet whispers between my grassy banks
Rippling over stones worn smooth by my soft presence
To sparkle with light in the afternoon sun
and give visual to the magic of my dance
I'd tickle the nose of furry friends
who stop by for a taste of life
And under the silvery light of a crescent moon
I hope lovers dip their toes

The Exchange

Wind it blows a wicked note and takes night's deafening silence
Want and need battle for a soul that hangs preciously in the balance
Screams of feral lust and love split through time to prove life is eternal
then eyes see color in the dark of night and essence leads the way
the universe opens her waiting arms to give and take the
highest energy
love

Fit

I don't fit your fucking narrative…fuck you. You can't make me something else because you'd like it better. Because it fits your story. If you can't see how truly badass I am, you were never worthy of me. Level up or fall back.

Little Badass

Skinny little thing with mousy brown hair in a haphazard ponytail. Everything about her is disheveled. Clothes a bit baggy and looking all messy. She isn't even a little shy. She's friendly with a pretty little smile and doesn't hesitate to ask for what she needs. I can't help but wonder what her life is like. She seems happy and confident, so I hope her life is good, happy and safe. It probably it. But maybe she's a little warrior who has troubles her friends can't even imagine. She handles those woes and on she goes. I choose to believe her life is happy because that's the better thought but either way her eyes are the eyes of a little badass.

Beast

I lay spent. A sweaty, used mess. Heart pounding, lightheaded. I don't really feel the soreness yet but I'll feel it shortly and for a few days. I should go to the bathroom and clean my self, I feel the cum running down my ass, but I just lay here. Glowing on the inside. Close to peace. The beast in me quiet for a time. People think only men are beasts but be well informed, there is a long toothed, clawed animal caged only by soft skin and pretty clothes.

Glory

Lovers tangle in the night
The dance of love
The dance of life
While some enjoy fleeting moments of glory
Others bend time to transcend the common
To love with a passion so fierce others can only envy
Blood turns to lava consuming anything ordinary
Leaving behind a creature touched by the divine

Vapor

Vapor.
That's what I am
Just tiny particles disappearing on the wind
No one notices me
They don't see me
Who cares?
No one
Not even the Vapor

Lull Prayer

Well I've been holding on so tight
Just can't seem to trust the flight
Feels more like fallin' than soarin'
I just can't get this right
Wish I could catch the wind
That glides beneath these wings
I guess my fall from grace always had it's place
So I'll lick my wounds under the blue moon
Rest my head on the ground
To listen to the Earth's wild song
Lull me to sleep tonight
Beneath the twinkling light
Hold my soul close in arms built of peace
To let the weary seep from my bones
In my dreams let me lay in field of soft cotton
For my mind's not forgotten
The comfort of home
Left long ago to wander life alone
I miss the feel of home and the smell of love
In my dreams let laughter sing the sweet song of life
so that melody wraps a warm blanket around the cold
Lull me to sleep tonight
Beneath the twinkling light
Hold my soul close in arms built of love
To let the weary seep from my bones
Please
let the weary seep from my bones

Granny's Table

    I wish I could sit at my Granny's table. I'm sure it was modest. She was poor her whole life. Hell, I don't even remember the table or the dishes. I remember her cooking and putting the food out for us. She had a big flour bowl she mixed dough in. Didn't measure a thing. Just put it in and mixed until it was right. Made biscuits every day and usually cornbread too. Always, always had a pot of beans. Fried potatoes and Mackerel patties came around real often too. My granny had steel in her veins. Took no shit and gave no shit. You best believe if she warned you, you need to heed. With only an 8th grade education she was smarter and wiser than most. Her eyes cut through the lard of life before others had time to turn the idea over in their head. And at her table I ate for my belly and took in food for my mind and nourishment for my soul. I sat there and watched her nurture her family and cut low people who dared mess with them. And let me tell you. I was her favorite. I could do no wrong. And when it was just us, as often it was when I was very young, she let me sing at the table. The only person who ever wanted to hear me sing. That's a real testament to how much she loved me. Lord I wish I could sit at my Granny's table.
(being my granny's favorite was strictly in my mind. My cousins would probably say they were her favorite too lol)

?

If my soul cried out in crippling despair, would it be heard?
Would it be answered?
Held in absolute love.
Sheltered like the most precious thing.
Or do I go unheard?

Elixir

And the taste of thee it makes me three
Sweet and tangy you tingle my tongue
Rich and earthy your boutique fills my nose
Why did I drink of your intoxicating elixir
for it's the taste of you I crave night and day

Light the Night

    Beautiful bridges burn too. They burn just as easily as any other bridge. You might think it's a shame because of it's beauty but in the end it's just a pile of ash. Whatever was remarkable, whatever caused that beauty, is gone in the end. And the heat from that beautiful bridge is no different from an ugly truth that burned before. I suppose if there's any difference at all it's in the very beginning. When the flames first lick the posts. Or maybe it's just before collapse, fully engulfed and completely consumed. Each can say when it's the loveliest.

In His Eyes

In his eyes I'm an angel
My horns form a halo to shine bright and light his way
He doesn't see the stain of blood that holds to every crack and crevice
In his eyes I fly on beautiful white wings
Soft and lovely he sees me floating in time
If he looked through another's eyes he'd see white hot heat at my back
An inferno I barely cage
In his eyes my skin is soft and lovely
And yields to his strong touch
Without the scales that protect my hateful bones and guts
My armor grey and black and hard as stone I'd like to shed this skin
Begin again
When I gaze at my reflection I try so hard to see
The version of me that he sees
But I see the demon who plays in greys
Who keeps time in lovely sin
There are 3 shes.
The she the world sees
The she I see
The she he sees

What Spills From Me

What song is that the wind sings? A haunting melody that takes me to another place. A place where nightmares become dreams become reality.

It appeared to be a rabid beast I fought but it was only me. Once I could see I became blind to the rest my eyes no longer searching for devils in the dark. There's no need the devil lies in me.

And so upon the fertile ground I bleed, a life, a love, too big to see. Only one knows it's me. Only one sees what spills from me.

What She was Given

      She looks across her field marveling at the gifts she'd been given. Each one a precious wonder of life. "How lucky" she thinks as she smells the air, "to have this." The warmth came from every direction. The top of her head, the soles of her feet and all points in between. Butterflies flutter softly around her in a sweet blessing dance. One by one they come to share in her love. To feel the warmth as she does. Finally, when night falls, in her lover's arms she lets the darkness have her. For all the beauty the day held strong the night is where her heart belongs. Where lightening bugs dot the lovely field and the wolf answers her call. Then hot blue fire licks orange to the heavens and desire pounds thunderous in the night. All is lost save only her lust for life. As she lays quiet upon his chest, a smile playing mischievous across her lips having found peace once more, she licks his skin to taste him once again.

My Body

My body tells my story
It tells my time
It tells my choices
I could look in the mirror and wish for youth but I don't
I could look in the mirror and wish I'd eaten well
and that I do
but not because I dislike what I see but more because I value me

Time

Time is a measure we need not heed
Live for this moment
Revisit the past but don't live there
Look to future moments with hope
But don't tarry too long and miss this moment
This one
This
one

Fucking People

We're such wasteful shits
Wasting food
Wasting money
Wasting minds
Wasting time

Ailments of the Human Condition

This need is chronically acute
Always there
Always intense
I think to ease the ache just a little
Only to make my condition worse
There is no bandage for what ails me
No simple surgery to be sought
I'll apply a little pressure and
Let nature run it's course

Rain

Splat a Tat Tat
I hear the rain beating down
It keeps a different rhythm than you
You're slow and torturous
Drawing my pleasure out with each long stroke
My breathing so heavy
Fog covers the windows
Muscles in your arms and back strain and tighten and
Radiate energy beneath my fingertips
Your kisses both soft and feverish scorch burns across my neck
The rain beats slower than you now as you pound a faster beat
Tense and strung tight I hold on for pure life
Losing my own rhythm
Ecstasy takes flight

Simple People

    I envy simple people. The ones who see only what they want instead of what is. The ones with all the answers to every question never asked of them. The ones with ideas so serious they become a motto then never wonder another thought. The ones who see only black and white instead color's light. Such a simple little world they have. It surely must be bliss.

The Cover of Night

What is it about the cover of night that gives people permission?
Makes them feel safe to be a little risqué.
Allows the meek a measure of boldness.
What is it about the cover of night that tells some to be naughty when they try so hard for well behaved?
But the call of the wild won't be silenced forever
It can't be
Nature can't be denied
Why even try?
My friends, you don't need the moon's permission to play

My Love

What if my love isn't a spring bloom to blossom for it's season in beautiful glory only to fade in the fall. What if my love is Pando? Old and great. A genet of glorious golden life bursting upward so old and strong and steady with roots vast and deep. A crown upon the Earth. Some loves are pretty little things and others are…other.

Lovely is the Day

Lovely is the day spent in the company of love
Where it's beautiful in the sun and rain alike
Lovely is the day spent on the company of love
Where breaking bread with a special person is more than just a meal
Lovely is the day spent in the company of love
Walking arm in arm the journey the true destination
Lovely is the day spent in the company of love
Speaking with a beautiful mind full of color, knowledge and fun
Lovely is the day spent in the company of you

21 Day Challenge

My cousin and I did a 21 day challenge together where we wrote something every day. This was a little more challenging than I thought it would be as you might see in these following writings.

Day 1
Hell has a new Boss
Can I sit with you on your paper moon
The sky is sorta pretty with your make-believe stars
We can watch the world together maybe giggle in glee
at the pitiful pretend people below
When we're tired of the show
I'll tie string around my toe and use the other end for a lasso
To Hitch a ride on the great white horse as he flies by
With tight rein I'll drive him straight and low
And wave prettily to all as I charge the beast heavily through the gates of Hell
That's what monsters do

Day 2
      Sitting on the front steps had lost its appeal. I sat there just the same in the August sun, as I had in July and June and months before and years before that. I looked at the grass, it still grew green. I watched a small yellow butterfly float by and knew it probably wasn't the same one but it was familiar in way i could almost connect. Almost. The sun was still hot and the breeze still lifted my hair but it was all so distant. Somehow the moment should be vivid, bursting with life but it was dull and grey. Oh the sky was so blue, it was easy to see that much but it felt grey as fuck. The sun warmed my skin but couldn't reach my soul. Some piece of me was lost, or hidden, or misplaced. That's it. I was displaced

Day 3

    That boy didn't see me. Hell none of them do. I sit here with a smile, making small talk with a nit wit. She's a nice nit wit but with the depth of a barely formed mud puddle. It's comical really. Listening to her chatter on about her new shoes. I do the same. It's easy. Easy to pretend those kinds of things matter to me. Meanwhile, as my eyes sparkle seemingly from the love of shoes and my glossy lips curl into a smile she thinks is for her witty comments the reel in my mind plays a scene with his hands firmly on my wrists, pinned to the wall. The sound of feral need rattling around in my head. Not one of these people know a beast sits with them. Breaks bread like a common person. I chuckle to myself, how easy it is.

Day 4

    Do you ever wonder who's feet walked your ground before you? Or the ground beneath pavement you're currently stomping. I mean this literally. Often I'm walking, step after step, around the yard, in town, on a trail and I wonder who walked this ground before me. Who walked it earlier today? Is their life ok for the most part? Who walked it 20 years ago, 50 years, 100, 200? Who were they? What did they leave of themselves? This always leads me to wonder who will walk it after me? What will I leave of me?

Day 5
The Pull
I didn't know i could be tethered without the first restraint
No bindings to hold me to a spot but some sort of invisible thread
Winding and twining it's way around me
Delicate and lovely, spun out of air but with the strength of steel it pulls at me
My will has no matter here the pull has it's own
Fighting gains me little but bruises
In surrender I find the weightless bliss of floating on warm air

Day 6
Shadows are a beautiful thing.
You can't have one without the light
A place of darkness created by light isn't that really a great representation of life
The balance of life
They're a place to hide
A place to wonder what's hiding
A place to rest
A place to play
Do you love the night?
Don't get me wrong I love my time in the light
But when the shadow is cast I pull it around me like the softest cloak and savor what is mine

Day 7
What's lost?
      Pretend just for a minute that everything man-made, manufactured, is gone. We all just woke up on the ground naked without the first thing. Where would we start? How long would it take us to build back? Could we build back?
We've lost so much knowledge I wonder how many could even survive?

Day 8
      Sitting sideways in my window nook I watched the weeds blow in the breeze thinking how normal that is. How easy that is. To just go with the flow. And usually I do just go with the flow but not today. Today I'll rip someone apart. Today I'll tear that person's world apart. No, she did that to herself, really. I'm just the one to see it through

Day 9
I whisper my secrets to the ether
I give them to the Gods
So when my soul is sucked into the void
there's nothing for the monsters to eat

Day 10
Scarred
My skin is rough
you made it that way
Does it please you?
My heart is hollow
Are you proud?
My bones are fire forged steel
And I thank you for that
When I'm cut
I barely bleed
I have nothing left to give
I am your Frankenstein

Day 11
I'm cold to the bone
Can't catch even a memory of heat
It'd be wise to cross the street when we meet
I'm cutting people like ripe burley
Swift swing
Moving on
I don't even care enough to spear
Just leaving you there to rot

Day 12

A beautiful, golden butterfly with blue eyes caught my sight.
I watched that little yellow thing flutter about
Flower to flower
I could swear I heard it laughing
Merrily here and there it did go
And I couldn't help but walk to the daisy it sat upon
But just as I got to that daisy that pretty yellow butterfly flew to another
A little faster I walked to the next
But again that butterfly flew to another flower
Even faster I went to the next
And faster again to the next
I watched the pretty yellow thing fly higher
I ran fast
It flew higher and farther
I ran faster
It flew higher and farther
I ran faster
With my smiling face pointed straight to the sky I ran right off the cliff

Day 13

The smell invades my head
Burns down my throat like acid
Memories blaze through my mind like wildfire
I'd cut you from my gut if I could
I wrap my cold black soul around your warmth
A pitiful attempt to smother you out
To invade you with my seething darkness
Still you persist
Ever hot

Burning hot as you might be
You will not melt me

Day 14
Asleep Awake floating on a boat made of air
I drift across an ocean of bliss
Rocked back and forth and back again
No time
No space
No room for plans
Just lovely blue water

Day 15
I'll go quietly into the night
You don't have to worry I'll make a scene
I won't key your car
Or flatten your tires
I won't take back gifts I gave in love
I won't throw your things out the door
I won't make shitty "hate you" posts
I won't wish you ill
I won't scream at you
In fact I don't believe you'll even know I'm gone
But one day when you don't see me
And you miss my quiet presence
And you're somehow less without me
You'll morn the ghost of me

Day 16
Visitor in my own life

Nothing seems as it should
A parasite in my own skin
Seems I should be able to dig my way out
How did I get left out of my own life?
Or left behind?
Or did I grow forward faster that I can keep up with?
I don't know
But here I stand a stranger in my own mind
Every person I see, every building I cross, even the ground and sky are distorted
Mocking

Day 17

How can my head be so loud and so void
I didn't know I was a firebug but in my mind I burned a church. I was just tired of it so I lit the match
And when I'm riding down the road, I don't want to stop. I just wanna drive until I hit saltwater
Maybe I'll just sit in my van awhile
Close my eyes and wish myself away
I'm not ungrateful, I'm really not, I'm just tired
And restless
And longing

Day 18

I seem to have an endless supply of flesh and blood
I take lash after lash after lash
I don't bleed out
I just feel the sting
See red

And it happens all over again
Did someone teach you just how to cut me
To bleed me but not kill me
Did someone school you in the art of my torture
Did someone lay that knowledge at your feet and now you wear it as a well formed boot to kick me
Yes
I suppose someone did
I reckon it was me

Day 19

Loneliness is a quiet, invasive vine until its rooted deep in your feet
And wrapped tightly around your heart leaving only little patches of surface still seeking not be lonely
But now the heart is too covered in the dark ivy to even know with certainty that another heart is near
But foolish as a heart will be it pushes against that vine
Trying to feel for something else
Hoping not to be alone
But that wretched fucking vine squeezes harder and cuts deeper
Growing in the dark

Day 20

It don't hurt to know people.
Who do I know...
I have a friend or 2 who are wealthy, they don't seem to mind I'm not.
I have a friend who's a heroin addict, she doesn't try to pull me in
I have some friends who lean heavily on their religion yet they still friend this heathen, I'm sure I get some prayers

I have a friend or 2 very similar to me in many ways and that's not so easy to find
I have some homosexual friends, they don't mind I'm straight
I know people who've spent time behind bars, some of the best
I know people who've served our country and I appreciate every one. I hope I don't disappoint them when I take my freedom for granted
I know talented wonderful people with gifts not everyone has
I know good strong trustworthy people
I know people you can't trust an inch
Who do you know?

Day 21
When I hit the end of this bottle I won't feel so tight
The world's gonna be a little fuzzy but that's just right
I drink to the Gods and Demons alike
And dance with one of each tonight
When I hit the end of this bottle I'll see the world through amber glasses
And be happy to stand about with the wretched masses
Laughing at fools falling on their asses
When I hit the end of the bottle all I'll know is fun
I'll take my hair down out this bun
Stick a fork in me this challenge is done.

Day 21 again (just because)
It fits me perfectly
It's weight I don't even feel
Shinning bright gold on fire shaped tips of obsidian
It marks my station
A show of power
I don't need it but I like it

I wear my crown to feast

To survey the gardens

To pass judgements

To dance

To decide the course of my people

To pick fabrics

Even to take a royal shit

At night I lay it to rest upon an emerald satin pillow covered by a cloth of the just same

When the sun kisses my face again I'll don my beautiful crown

To rule the world for another day

Author Bio

I'm just a person who likes to empty my mind on paper and canvas. I'm truly honored and appreciate you reading my book. Thank you.

Rhonda has writings in:
'Memories Worth Remembering'
'Potpourri 2 Every Flavor of Short Story"

Works also found on lulu.com

Please visit Fair Fine Art on fb and Instagram
You can contact Rhonda by email at rhonda@fairfineart.com

www.ingramcontent.com/pod-product-compliance
Lightning Source LLC
Chambersburg PA
CBHW060847050426
42453CB00008B/869